KITTEN CARE
AND CRITTERS, TOO!

**Judy Petersen-Fleming
and Bill Fleming**

Photographs by Debra Reingold-Reiss

Tambourine Books
New York

This book is dedicated to all the people who devote their lives to the care and well-being of animals. It's also for all those children who will grow up to choose lifestyles and careers and do the same.

ACKNOWLEDGMENTS

Our most sincere appreciation to the institutions that supplied the critter photographs. We applaud their commitment to educating the public about the animals and their habitats that we call the wild kingdom.

At Marine World Africa U.S.A., Vallejo, California, special thanks to Mary O'Herron, Darryl Bush, and Jim Bonde, who have been extraordinary to work with, and to the devoted people that care for their animals: John Long, Steve Nagle, Mary Fleming, Mark Jardarian, Andy Goldfarb, J.R., and Kim and Liam Hussey.

At San Diego Zoo, San Diego, California, very special thanks to Jeff Jouett and Laurie Krusinski for all their help, and to the dedicated keepers: Elaine Chu, Craig Rasicot, and Amy Kendall.

At Sea World, Orlando, Florida, we'd like to acknowledge Jack Pearson and Toni Caracciolo for all the time and help they gave us, and to thank animal care specialists Amy Perry and Jeff Basso.

At Sea World, San Diego, California, thanks to Margaret Retzlaff for her patience and ready help at any given time, and to the people whose care for the animals is reflected in the photographs throughout this book: Mark Bressler and Burke Stillick.

Special thanks to renowned veterinarian Kevin T. Fitzgerald, D.V.M.

Thanks also to all the organizations whose mission is to find homes for orphaned animals, some of whom are featured throughout this book: Animal Orphanage, Colorado Humane Society and SPCA, The Cat Care Society, Denver Dumb Friends League—Humane Society of Denver, Inc., Intermountain Humane Society, Max Fund Adoption Center, and Save An Animal Foundation.

NOTE TO PARENTS:

Raising a kitten can be a wonderful experience for a child as well as the whole family. Whether you read to your son or daughter, or your child

reads to younger siblings, the easy-care methods described in this book will help your children feel pride in caring for their pet.

The keepers and trainers of the exotic animals feel the same way, as you will discover throughout this book. It's never too soon to teach our children respect for animals— whether they are the ones we keep at home or the ones we visit in zoos. While providing love and proper care to a pet, children will begin to understand and appreciate all animals much more.

When your family is ready to choose a new companion don't forget to go to the local animal shelter first. The many orphaned cats and kittens make the best pets!

Now that you have decided to bring a kitten home you will want to know how to take care of it. There are a few important things to learn that will keep your new kitten healthy and make him a happy member of your family.

Throughout this book you will also see the keepers and trainers in wild animal parks taking care of their animals. They are doing just what you are learning to do.

Don't forget that a happy, healthy pet is fun to have around.

A KITTEN SHOULD NOT BE SEPARATED FROM ITS MOTHER FOR AT LEAST SEVEN WEEKS.

When you go to choose your kitten from the local pound or a litter, pick a healthy kitten. Check the kitten's eyes, nose, and ears; they should be clear and clean.

You also want to find a friendly kitten. You can determine how friendly a kitten is by watching each one carefully. Bring a piece of yarn to see if the kitten will play with it. Remember to move slowly so you don't scare the kittens.

AND CRITTERS, TOO!

Just like your new kitten, all of these young tiger cubs have their own personalities. Some can be timid and shy while others are playful and adventurous.

This trainer spends many hours a day with the cubs so he can get to know each one very well. By the time the tigers have grown up, he will understand each one and know how they will behave in any situation.

EACH TIGER'S SET OF STRIPES IS UNIQUE—JUST LIKE A PERSON'S FINGERPRINTS.

ALMOST ALL CATS HAVE A COAT OF SOFT FUR TO PROTECT THEM AND KEEP THEM WARM.

Now that you've picked your new kitten, you need to learn how to hold him, even before you take him home. When you pick up your kitten, never grab him by the legs or the head. You should scoop him up, supporting him with one hand under his tail end and the other under his chest. Be careful not to squeeze too tight!

A SEA OTTER'S FUR HAS MORE HAIRS PER SQUARE INCH THAN ANY OTHER ANIMAL'S IN THE WORLD.

This baby sea otter's trainer takes him to the clinic to get his vitamins. The trainer had to learn the proper way to hold and carry young otters.

9

YOU CAN TELL YOUR KITTEN IS FRIGHTENED WHEN HER EARS ARE FLAT AND HER EYES ARE ROUND.

Your kitten may be afraid of her new home at first. To keep her calm put her in a room that's warm and quiet, without a lot of places to hide. Try making a soft bed for your kitten from a towel or a folded blanket.

In the beginning, spend as much time as you can in the room with her. Just sit in one spot and let your kitten come to you. Soon she will start to feel very comfortable being near you.

AND CRITTERS, TOO!

Baby orangutan Kayla's first few nights in the nursery could have been scary for her, but her trainer put a soft blanket and stuffed animals next to her. Then she felt safer and more comfortable. During the night, the trainer stayed by her and patted her if she became afraid.

ORANGUTANS CAN GROW TO WEIGH OVER FOUR HUNDRED FIFTEEN POUNDS!

WHEN KITTENS ARE VERY SMALL, THEIR MOTHER CARRIES THEM GENTLY IN HER MOUTH.

Kittens take time! The first three months of your kitten's life are the most important time for your kitten to become part of your family.

A cat living in the wild depends on her mother for warmth, companionship, and to teach her to survive. Your new kitten will expect you and your family to do these same things.

After school and before you go play with your friends, it is important to give your new kitten a lot of time and attention. To do this you might have to give up other activities.

AND CRITTERS, TOO!

Her trainer has raised this baby penguin since she was hatched from an egg. The trainer spends time petting and talking calmly to her before he takes her to get weighed. Trainers know that giving time to the baby penguins when they are young makes them feel more secure and happy when they grow up.

A PENGUIN'S ENTIRE BODY IS COVERED WITH FEATHERS TIGHTLY PRESSED TOGETHER THAT KEEP THE PENGUIN WARM.

CATS ARE MEAT EATERS. THEY HAVE ONLY THIRTY TEETH, FEWER THAN ANY OTHER MEAT-EATING MAMMAL.

Your kitten will depend on you to make sure she is cared for and fed daily. You can share this job with your younger brother or sister so they will feel part of caring for your kitten, too.

Let them pour the dry food into the bowl. Your parents can also help you pick what kind of food your kitten needs and how much.

When this orphaned koala, Pulyara, was first born, her keepers had to make sure she was getting the best diet to help her grow properly.

A wild koala's mother only eats eucalyptus leaves. Her keepers feed Pulyara a special formula made from different kinds of food. The veterinarian created this formula to include all the same vitamins that are in her mother's milk.

KOALA MEANS "BEAR WITH A LEATHER BAG." ACTUALLY, KOAL ARE NOT RELATED TO BEARS AT ALL, AND THE "LEATHER BAG" IS THE POUCH WHERE THEY CARRY THEIR YOUNG LIKE KANGAROOS.

CATS CAN'T SWEAT LIKE PEOPLE DO TO COOL OFF. THE ONLY PARTS ON A CAT'S BODY THAT CAN SWEAT ARE HER PAWS.

It is very important that your kitten always has some water to drink. It can be dangerous to your kitten's health if he ever overheats and stays thirsty for a long period of time.

Place a full bowl of water near the area where your kitten eats. Keep a full bowl outside, too, and check the bowls often to make sure they are full.

AND CRITTERS, TOO!

This baby gazelle's mother didn't take care of her, so a keeper took over. He always makes sure that Ginger has water so she won't overheat and get sick.

GAZELLES HAVE ONE CALF AT A TIME. A CALF CAN ALREADY NURSE AND WALK ONLY THIRTY MINUTES AFTER BIRTH.

A CAT CAN TELL THE DIFFERENCE
BETWEEN A MOVING MOUSE
AND A MOVING LEAF OVER
FIFTY FEET AWAY—IN THE DARK.

Your kitten expects you to be her mother. (Yes, even boys will be "mom" to their kitten!) She will want you to teach her what she can and cannot do in her new home, just as her mother would in the wild.

18

AND CRITTERS, TOO!

Spike, a baby wallaby, rides in the pouch his trainer wears. It's just like being in his mother's pouch. Spike depends on the trainer to do all the things that his mother would do.

WALLABIES ARE PART OF THE KANGAROO FAMILY. THEY SPEND THE FIRST EIGHT MONTHS OF THEIR LIVES IN THEIR MOTHER'S POUCH. THEY DON'T EVEN POKE THEIR HEADS OUT OF THE POUCH UNTIL THEY ARE FIVE MONTHS OLD.

THE AVERAGE CAT CAN UNDERSTAND TWENTY-FIVE TO FIFTY WORDS.

This girl is teaching her kitten not to scratch, and to keep his claws in. She is telling him "no."

Teaching your kitten what "no" means is important from the beginning. Whenever your kitten is doing something he shouldn't, say a stern "no" to him. Always use the same word and the same tone of voice. It will confuse your kitten if you say other words like "don't" or "stop." And never yell "no." This will only frighten your kitten, and he cannot learn if he is afraid.

This trainer is telling the baby lion "no" after she playfully tried to take a nip at him.

Nikka learned the meaning of "no" when she was very young. Sometimes Nikka forgets. Then the trainer gently reminds her what "no" means.

LION CUBS ARE BORN WITH SPOTS THAT DISAPPEAR WHEN THEY GET OLDER.

WHEN YOUR KITTEN ARCHES HER BACK, SHE IS DISTRUSTFUL.

Keep your kitten in one room while she is being trained to use the litter box. Choose the room in which she is most comfortable.

After each meal, gently place her in the sand. Usually she will go potty naturally. If she doesn't, be patient until she does.

When your kitten uses her box, give her lots of praise and love. This teaches her that she has done what is right and will help her learn that her box is the only place to go to the bathroom.

AND CRITTERS, TOO!

This young tiger, Hobbes, learned to use his litter box when he was traveling around the country for education programs.

His trainers spent a lot of time with him when Hobbes was first learning to use the box. When baby Hobbes went potty in the box, the trainers praised him so he knew he'd done right, exactly like you do with your kitten!

TIGER CUBS WEIGH ONLY TWO OR THREE POUNDS AT BIRTH. THEY ARE BLIND AND DEAF WHEN THEY ARE BORN, JUST LIKE KITTENS.

**CATS GROOM THEMSELVES
VERY CAREFULLY.
THEY LICK THEMSELVES
CLEAN FROM THEIR HEADS
DOWN TO THEIR TAILS.**

Cleaning your cat's litter box needs to be done daily. The major reason a kitten will not use her litter box is because it is not clean. Cleaning is so easy to do! All you need is a scoop and a sack. Just push your scooper through the litter and throw all the material you find in the sack. Once a week replace the litter and clean the box.

Accidents can happen. If you catch your kitten going potty outside her litter box, say a stern "no" and put her in her litter box. Never yell at your kitten. That will only scare her and make her confused.

This keeper takes great pride in keeping the large area clean in which Nairobi, the baby giraffe, lives.

Nairobi is much happier and healthier when her home is nice and clean.

GIRAFFES' TONGUES CAN GROW OVER FIFTEEN INCHES LONG SO THEY CAN REACH LEAVES FROM

CATS CAN SLEEP UP TO EIGHTEEN HOURS A DAY.

Kittens need daily naps while they are growing and even when they are adults. You need to be careful that you don't over tire your kitten, so let him rest when he needs it. You might like to rest right next to your kitten while he is napping.

Being able to share quiet time together will make the two of you better friends. It will help him learn to feel content and safe around you.

These trainers know how important it is to spend quiet periods with these chimpanzees, Patti and Baby Thiele. During this special time the chimps can just relax and enjoy the trainers' company.

CHIMPANZEES LAUGH, JUST LIKE YOU DO.

YOU KNOW YOUR KITTEN IS CONTENT WHEN HER EARS ARE STRAIGHT UP AND HER EYES ARE ROUND.

During quiet time, when your kitten is nice and calm, you can gently stroke her. It is important to always use very slow, gentle movements with your hands. Fast hands can excite and confuse your kitten, making her think it's playtime instead of quiet time.

This keeper hand raised this baby trumpeter, Daffy. She learned to be very gentle when caring for Daffy by using a slow hand so Daffy didn't become excited.

GRAY-WINGED TRUMP

MALES MAKE A LOUD

TRUMPETING SOUND.

CATS HAVE POWERFUL
MUSCLES AND CAN LEAP
VERY HIGH.

Playtime is very important for your kitten. It helps your kitten keep fit, alert, and happy. Playing with your kitten will be loads of fun for both of you. You can spend many hours together making up different games.

30

This baby polar bear, Kiska, loves to play for several hours a day. She loves to roll around, jump from rock to rock, and chase her mother. Playtime helps Kiska keep fit while she is growing.

POLAR BEARS HAVE THOUSANDS OF FINE HAIR ON THE BOTTOMS OF THEIR FEET TO KEEP THEM WARM WHEN WALKING ON THE ICE.

CATS' SHARP CLAWS ARE HIDDEN IN THEIR PAWS AND COME OUT WHEN THEY NEED THEM.

Toys make playtime even more fun. Almost anything can be a toy for a kitten. Try playing chase with several Ping-Pong balls, or give your kitten an empty paper bag and watch the fun begin!

Never let your kitten use your hand as a toy. Your kitten can claw and bite any of his toys, but you must teach him that hands are off-limits during playtime.

AND CRITTERS, TOO!

Just like your kitten, this chimpanzee, Bobby, loves to play with all kinds of different toys. His favorite toys are stuffed animals and a play phone.

Bobby's trainers give him different toys every day, so he won't get bored always playing with the same ones.

CHIMPANZEES USE TOOLS TO HELP THEM GET FOOD TO EAT, LIKE PUSHING A STICK DOWN A HOLE TO FIND TERMITES.

A CAT HAS FIVE TOES ON EACH FRONT PAW, AND FOUR TOES ON EACH HIND PAW.

It will also be your job to help teach your younger brother or sister to be gentle with your new kitten. You can set an example by showing them how softly you handle your kitten.

AND CRITTERS, TOO!

These trainers were taught to be very careful and gentle, too, while caring for these orphaned baby manatees, who were rescued after their mothers died. The trainers work together to make sure that Little Joe and his friend are handled with great care, and that the manatees are always happy and healthy.

MANATEES LIVE IN THE WATER, BUT ARE RELATED TO ELEPHANTS.

YOU CAN TELL WHEN YOUR CAT IS HAPPY WHEN SHE WALKS WITH HER TAIL HELD HIGH IN THE AIR.

All the time and care you give to your kitten will make him happy to live with his caring family. You'll have a friend for life!

WHERE TO VISIT THE KEEPERS AND THEIR ANIMALS

MARINE WORLD AFRICA U.S.A.

MARINE WORLD PARKWAY

VALLEJO, CA 94589

FOR INFORMATION CALL:

(707) 644-4000

p. 7

p. 11

p. 19

p. 21

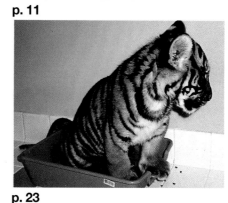
p. 23

p. 25

p. 27

p. 33

p. 15

p. 17

p. 29

SAN DIEGO ZOO

2920 ZOO DRIVE

SAN DIEGO, CA 92109

FOR INFORMATION

CALL: (619) 234-3153

p. 31

SEA WORLD OF FLORIDA

7007 SEA WORLD DRIVE

ORLANDO, FL 32821

FOR INFORMATION CALL:

(407) 363-2613

p. 35

p. 9

p. 13

SEA WORLD OF CALIFORNIA

1720 SOUTH SHORES ROAD

SAN DIEGO, CA 92109

FOR INFORMATION CALL:

(619) 226-3901

Library of Congress Cataloging in Publication Data
Petersen-Fleming, Judy. Kitten care and critters, too!/by Judy Petersen-Fleming and Bill Fleming;
photographs by Debra Reingold-Reiss. — 1st ed. p. cm. Summary: Explains how to choose, train,
and care for a kitten, with comparisons to other animals.
1. Kittens—Juvenile literature. 2. Animals—Juvenile literature. [1. Cats. 2. Pets.
3. Animals.] I. Fleming, Bill. II. Reingold-Reiss, Debra, ill. III. Title
SF445.7.P373 1994 636.8'07—dc20 93-24200 CIP AC
ISBN 0-688-12565-4 (trade). — ISBN 0-688-12566-2 (lib.)
1 3 5 7 9 10 8 6 4 2
First edition

PHOTO CREDITS

Cover photographs by Darryl Bush/Marine World Africa U.S.A., Vallejo, California.
Photographs on pages 7, 11, 19, 21, 23, 25, 27, and 33 copyright © 1994 by Marine
World Africa U.S.A., Vallejo, California.
Photographs on pages 9 and 13 copyright © 1994 by Sea World of California.
Photographs on pages 15, 17, 29, and 31 copyright © 1994 by the Zoological Society of San Diego.
Photograph on page 35 copyright © 1994 by Sea World of Florida.